BIGGEST NAMES IN MUSIC

TAYLOR SWIFT

by Emma Huddleston

T0014914

WWW.FOCUSREADERS.COM

Focus Readers is distributed by North Star Editions:
sales@northstareditions.com | 888-417-0195

Produced for Focus Readers by Red Line Editorial.

Photographs ©: Charles Sykes/Invision/AP Images, cover, 1; Chris Pizzello/Invision/AP Images, 4–5, 7, 24; Shutterstock Images, 8–9, 11, 13, 14–15, 17, 19, 20–21, 23, 29; Todd Williamson/Invision/AP Images, 26

Library of Congress Cataloging-in-Publication Data
Names: Huddleston, Emma, author.
Title: Taylor Swift / Emma Huddleston.
Description: Lake Elmo, MN : Focus Readers, 2021. | Series: Biggest names in
    music | Includes index. | Audience: Grades 4-6
Identifiers: LCCN 2020013669 (print) | LCCN 2020013670 (ebook) | ISBN
    9781644936405 (hardcover) | ISBN 9781644936498 (paperback) | ISBN
    9781644936672 (pdf) | ISBN 9781644936580 (ebook)
Subjects: LCSH: Swift, Taylor, 1989---Juvenile literature | Singers--United
    States--Biography--Juvenile literature. | Country musicians--United
    States--Biography--Juvenile literature.
Classification: LCC ML3930.S989 H84 2021 (print) | LCC ML3930.S989
    (ebook) | DDC 782.421642092 [B]--dc23
LC record available at https://lccn.loc.gov/2020013669
LC ebook record available at https://lccn.loc.gov/2020013670

Printed in the United States of America
Mankato, MN
082020

ABOUT THE AUTHOR

Emma Huddleston lives in the Twin Cities with her husband. She enjoys writing children's books and staying active. She thinks music is an important part of life and spends some afternoons learning how to play the piano.

TABLE OF CONTENTS

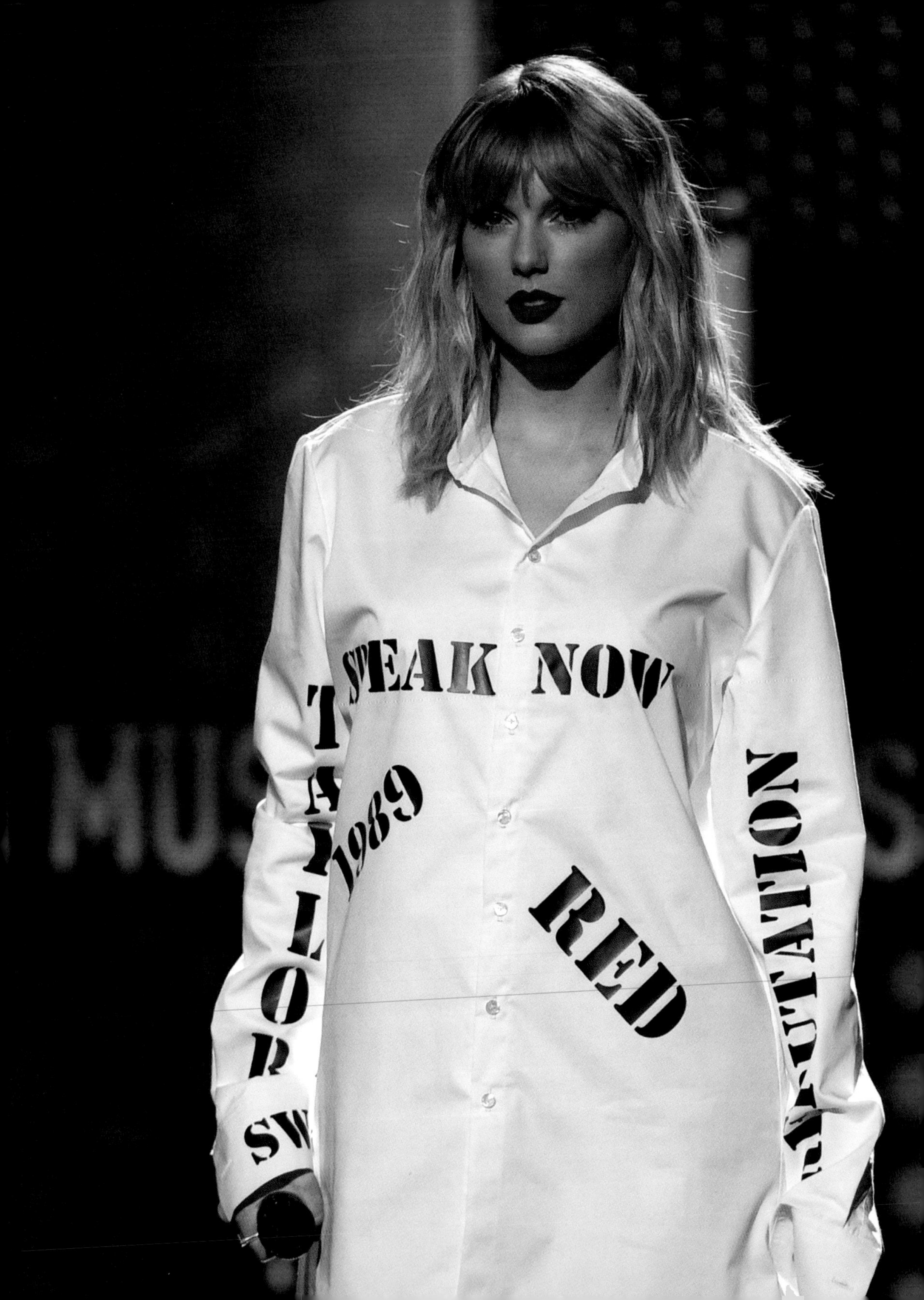
1989
RED

CHAPTER 1

RECORD BREAKER

Taylor Swift took the stage at the 2019 American Music Awards (AMAs). She had just been named Artist of the Decade. To celebrate, she performed a **medley** of some of her biggest hits.

For the first song, Swift wore a white button-down shirt. It had the titles of her albums printed in big black letters.

At the 2019 AMAs, Taylor Swift celebrated by singing her hit songs from the past 10 years.

A group of girls joined her onstage. They danced as Swift sang.

Next, Swift changed her costume to a sparkly gold leotard. She sang "Blank Space," "Shake It Off," and other big hits. Fans recognized each song after just a few notes. They cheered and sang along. A new group of dancers joined Swift for each song.

For the last song, Swift slowed the pace. She sat at a piano and wore a long, pink cape that draped onto the floor. She sang "Lover," a song from her newest album. Two ballet dancers twirled across the stage. When the song ended, the crowd burst into applause once more.

Camila Cabello (left) and Halsey (right) joined Swift onstage at the 2019 AMAs.

Swift won six AMAs that night. That brought her total to 29, which was more than any other artist. Once again, Swift proved her place as one of the biggest pop stars in the world.

CHAPTER 2

MAKING MUSIC

Taylor Alison Swift was born on December 13, 1989, in Reading, Pennsylvania. She and her brother grew up on a Christmas tree farm. Taylor was drawn to music from a young age. At age 10, she sang in local fairs and contests. Soon after, she learned to play guitar. By age 12, she was writing her own songs.

Taylor sings at California's Stagecoach Music Festival in 2008.

Taylor hoped to become a professional musician. She took trips with her family to Nashville, Tennessee. This city is known for country music. Many country singers start their careers there. Taylor hoped to get a **record deal**.

Her first tries were not successful. But she kept going back. When Taylor was 13, her family moved to Hendersonville, a town near Nashville. That way, the family wouldn't have to travel as far.

Taylor's breakthrough came when she was 14. She performed at the Bluebird Cafe in 2004. This cafe was known for its live music. People in the music business often went there to listen.

The Bluebird Cafe opened in 1982. Since then, many new artists and famous musicians have performed there.

Scott Borchetta heard Taylor's performance. Borchetta ran Big Machine Records. He thought Taylor was talented. Before long, he offered her a record deal with his company.

Taylor released her first **single**, "Tim McGraw," in June 2006. The song reached the Top 10 on country music charts. It also appeared on her first album, *Taylor Swift*. Taylor was 16 years old when this album came out in October 2006.

RECORD CONFLICT

Taylor Swift worked with Big Machine Records from 2006 to 2018. In that time, she released six albums. In November 2018, she began working with Republic Records instead. This split caused drama. Big Machine owned the rights to Swift's songs. That meant Big Machine could decide how and when the songs were used. Swift accused the company of limiting when she could perform some songs. Both sides claimed the other owed them money.

By 2009, Taylor had collected several ACM Awards, including Album of the Year.

The young singer released even more hits the next year. Then she won the Academy of Country Music (ACM) Award for Top New Female Vocalist. Her career was taking off.

CHAPTER 3

COUNTRY ROOTS

Swift began her rise to fame as a country star. But her catchy music appealed to a wide range of listeners. People were drawn to the stories she told through her songs. Her music often played on pop radio stations, not just country stations.

Swift performs in New York City in 2010.

Swift released *Fearless* in 2008. This second album was even more popular than her first. It topped both the country and pop charts for 11 weeks. Swift played songs from it on her first tour.

"Love Story" and "You Belong with Me" were especially big hits. In 2009, "You Belong with Me" won Best Female Video

HONEST SONGS

Swift quickly became known for her honest **lyrics**. She often writes about her life. Her songs tell her thoughts and feelings. They often talk about real people and events. Swift writes about both happiness and heartbreak. Many fans find her songs easy to relate to. They have felt similar emotions.

Swift won four Grammys for her album *Fearless* in 2010.

at the MTV Video Music Awards (VMAs). Until then, no country musician had ever won a VMA. And "Love Story" topped *Billboard*'s Pop Songs chart. This was rare for a country song.

In January 2010, *Fearless* won Album of the Year at the Grammys. Swift was just 20 years old. She set a new record as the youngest person to win that award. Artists are lucky to win even one Grammy. But Swift won four in that year alone. And her fame continued to grow.

Swift released a third album, *Speak Now*, in October. It topped charts around the world. The songs "Back to December" and "Mean" were especially popular. Their music videos got millions of views.

Swift also began changing her musical style. Her next album, *Red*, had more of a pop sound. **Critics** weren't sure she would have success in this new **genre**. But she

For her fourth album, *Red*, Swift began using instruments and beats more common in pop music.

proved them wrong. Tickets for some of her concerts sold out in less than two minutes.

CHAPTER 4

POP SUPERSTAR

In the mid-2010s, Swift proved she could be a pop superstar. Her next album, *1989*, came out in October 2014. It sold more than 1.2 million copies in the first week. By January 2015, it had gone platinum four times. Going platinum means selling more than one million copies.

Swift's new style was a hit with fans. Five songs from *1989* reached the Top 10 on *Billboard*'s charts.

In May, Swift began her tour for the album. She was so popular that most shows took place in huge stadiums. The stadiums could hold tens of thousands of people. Even so, most of the 83 shows sold out. Some also set records for attendance.

With such a strong fan base, Swift was free to experiment. She surprised fans by releasing the single "Look What You Made Me Do" in August 2017. It was part of the album *Reputation*, which came out in November.

Like Swift's other albums, *Reputation* went platinum. However, it also changed Swift's image. The album art and music

Swift's fans filled Wembley Stadium in London, England, during her *Reputation* tour in 2018.

videos featured black and red colors. They showed Swift as fierce. This was a big change from Swift's previous style. In the past, she often chose soft colors and had a sweet, smiling **persona**.

Swift sings "Me!" with Brendon Urie at the Billboard Music Awards in 2019.

In August 2019, Swift released her seventh album, *Lover.* This was her first album made with Republic Records. *Lover* had both country songs and pop songs.

It also returned to the bright, cheerful mood of her earlier music.

Throughout her long career, Swift has focused on helping others. In 2013, she opened the Taylor Swift Education Center in Nashville. Its classrooms and exhibits are part of the Country Music Hall of Fame. These spaces help children learn about music. Swift wanted to give back to the place where her career started.

Swift also gives money to people in need. She has donated money to cities for flood recovery. She has helped fans pay for school or hospital bills.

Early in her career, Swift didn't talk much about politics or social issues.

Swift performs in a concert for Breast Cancer Awareness Month.

Later, however, she began speaking out. In 2014 and 2015, for example, she challenged Spotify and Apple Music for not paying artists fairly. She didn't let these companies **stream** her music until they agreed to pay musicians more.

As one of the world's most successful singers, Swift uses her fame to talk about things she believes are important. Fans are eager to see what she will do next.

TELLING HER STORY

A documentary about Swift's life came out in 2020. It was called *Miss Americana*. In the movie, Swift talked openly about her music career and her life offstage. She admitted she struggled with an eating disorder. Swift talked about her unhealthy relationship with food in the past. She shared what helped her develop a better body image. She hoped fans with similar struggles could learn from her experience.

TAYLOR SWIFT

- Birth date: December 13, 1989
- Birthplace: Reading, Pennsylvania
- Family members: Andrea (mother), Scott (father), Austin (brother)
- High school: Aaron Academy
- Major accomplishments:
  - May 2007: Swift wins the ACM Award for Top New Female Vocalist.
  - September 2009: "You Belong with Me" makes Swift the first country musician to win a VMA.
  - January 2010: Swift wins four Grammys.
  - November 2011: Swift wins Artist of the Year at the AMAs for the second time.
  - February 2016: Swift wins three Grammys.
  - November 2019: Swift wins six AMAs, including Artist of the Decade.

Swift plays guitar during a show in Rio de Janeiro, Brazil, in December 2009.

- Quote: "If you just focus on the work and you don't let [people who try to take credit for your accomplishments] sidetrack you, someday [you'll succeed and] know it was you and the people who love you who put you there. And that will be the greatest feeling in the world."

Carolyn L. Todd. "Taylor Swift's Grammys Speech Inspires a Powerful Video About Girls in Music." *Refinery29*. Vice Media Group, 31 Jan. 2017. Web. 6 Apr. 2020.

FOCUS ON
TAYLOR SWIFT

Write your answers on a separate piece of paper.

1. Write a paragraph describing one of Swift's albums and how it changed her career.

2. If you became famous, would you want a documentary to be made about your life? Why or why not?

3. What was the name of Swift's second album?

   A. *Fearless*
   B. *Speak Now*
   C. *Red*

4. How did Swift's refusal to stream her music help create change?

   A. It showed that the streaming companies were not important to musicians.
   B. It showed that Swift's songs were not worth much money.
   C. Streaming companies wanted Swift's songs, so they agreed to pay musicians more.

Answer key on page 32.

GLOSSARY

critics
People who review music and give their thoughts on it.

genre
A category of music, such as rock, pop, or country.

lyrics
The words of a song.

medley
A musical piece that combines parts of several different songs.

persona
The way a person looks or behaves, as well as how this makes others think about that person.

record deal
An agreement where an artist makes an album that a company sells and promotes.

single
A song that is released on its own.

stream
To play videos or music by sending information over the internet.

TO LEARN MORE

BOOKS

Lajiness, Katie. *Taylor Swift*. Minneapolis: Abdo Publishing, 2016.

Morreale, Marie. *Taylor Swift: Born to Sing!* New York: Children's Press, 2017.

National Geographic Kids. *Turn It Up! A Pitch-Perfect History of Music That Rocked the World*. Washington, DC: National Geographic Kids, 2019.

NOTE TO EDUCATORS

Visit **www.focusreaders.com** to find lesson plans, activities, links, and other resources related to this title.

INDEX

Answer Key: **1.** Answers will vary; **2.** Answers will vary; **3.** A; **4.** C